THE RAINFOREST AND FRIENDS

By Stacie Groser and
Alissa Braun
Illustrated by Michael Magpantay

Library For All Ltd.

LIBRARY FOR ALL

DIGITAL EDUCATION

FOR THE WORLD

Library For All is an Australian not for profit organisation with a mission to make knowledge accessible to all via an innovative digital library solution. Visit us at libraryforall.org

The Rainforest and Friends

This edition published 2022

Published by Library For All Ltd
Email: info@libraryforall.org
URL: libraryforall.org

Library For All gratefully acknowledges the contributions of all who made previous editions of this book possible.

Original illustrations by Michael Magpantay

The Rainforest and Friends
Groser, Stacie and Braun, Alissa
ISBN: 978-1-922827-87-6
SKU02691

THE RAINFOREST AND FRIENDS

A forest is filled
with towering trees,
descending rain, and a
vast array of animals
and insects.

There's a special kind of forest called a tropical rainforest.

Rainforests make up
about five percent
of the Earth.

However, they are
home to millions of
plants and animals.

With so many
living things, there's
something new to see
around every corner.

9

There are toucans,

jaguars,

even spider monkeys.

There are lots of insects, such as the morpho butterfly and the rhinoceros beetle.

There are waterfalls.

And vines hanging
from trees.

Pretty sights around
every corner.

Animals moving throughout

and water dripping
down every crack.

Even at night when
most are at rest,

the rainforest is bursting with life.

You can use these questions to talk about this book with your family, friends and teachers.

What did you learn from this book?

Describe this book in one word. Funny? Scary? Colourful? Interesting?

How did this book make you feel when you finished reading it?

What was your favourite part of this book?

download our reader app
getlibraryforall.org

About the contributors

Library For All works with authors and illustrators from around the world to develop diverse, relevant, high quality stories for young readers. Visit libraryforall.org for the latest news on writers' workshop events, submission guidelines and other creative opportunities.

Did you enjoy this book?

We have hundreds more expertly curated original stories to choose from.

We work in partnership with authors, educators, cultural advisors, governments and NGOs to bring the joy of reading to children everywhere.

Did you know?

We create global impact in these fields by embracing the United Nations Sustainable Development Goals.

www.ingramcontent.com/pod-product-compliance
Lightning Source LLC
Chambersburg PA
CBHW040313050426
42452CB00018B/2826